Shadows of

Unveiling the

Christophe

2023

Note: This book aims to provide an objective and informative exploration of the Dark Web, shedding light on its various aspects, including its history, technologies, content, and societal implications. It is important to approach this subject matter responsibly and with the understanding that engaging in illegal activities or promoting harm is neither condoned nor encouraged.

Chapter 1: Into the Abyss: An Introduction to the Dark Web

Defining the Dark Web: Understanding its structure, purpose, and anonymity

The dark web is a hidden part of the internet that is not indexed by traditional search engines and requires specific software or configurations to access. It is often associated with illicit activities, anonymity, and secrecy. However, it is essential to note that the dark web serves various purposes, and not all its users engage in illegal activities. Understanding the structure and purpose of the dark web involves exploring its underlying technologies and the motivations of its users.

Structure of the Dark Web

- Overlay Networks: The dark web relies on overlay networks such as Tor (The Onion Router), I2P (Invisible Internet Project), and Freenet. These networks facilitate anonymous communication and routing by encrypting and bouncing internet traffic through multiple relays.
- Hidden Services: Within the dark web, websites and services operate as hidden services, utilizing .onion domains (in the case of Tor) or similar mechanisms. These websites are designed to provide anonymity to both visitors and operators by concealing the physical location of the server.
- Peer-to-Peer Networks: Some dark web platforms utilize peer-to-peer networks, allowing users to connect directly with each other without centralized servers. This further enhances privacy and decentralization.

Purposes and Activities on the Dark Web

- Privacy and Anonymity: The dark web offers a refuge for individuals seeking privacy in regions with oppressive regimes or surveillance. It provides an avenue for whistleblowers, activists, journalists, and dissidents to communicate and share sensitive information.
- Free Speech and Censorship Resistance: Some users value the dark web as a platform for unrestricted expression, where they can voice controversial opinions without fear of censorship or repercussions.
- Research and Information Sharing: Academic researchers, journalists, and cybersecurity professionals may utilize the dark web to study cybercriminal activities, monitor trends, and gather intelligence.
- Illicit Marketplaces: One significant aspect of the dark web is the presence of black markets, where illegal goods and services are traded. This includes drugs, weapons, stolen data, counterfeit currency, hacking tools, and more.
- Cybercrime and Hacking: The dark web provides a platform for cybercriminals to exchange information, sell stolen data, and offer hacking services.
- Extremism and Radical Ideologies: Some extremist groups and individuals exploit the dark web to disseminate propaganda, recruit members, and coordinate activities away from the scrutiny of law enforcement.

It is important to note that while the dark web facilitates anonymity, it can also attract criminal elements. However, it would be an oversimplification to characterize the entire dark web as inherently nefarious. It is a complex and multifaceted network with diverse purposes and users, ranging from those seeking privacy and security to those engaged in illicit activities.

Tracing the origins: From the birth of the internet to the emergence of the darknet

The origins of the dark web can be traced back to the development of the internet itself and the desire for privacy and anonymity in online communication. Several key developments and technologies have contributed to the emergence of the dark web as we know it today. Here are some notable milestones in its origins:

- The Birth of the Internet:

In the 1960s, the Advanced Research Projects Agency Network (ARPANET) laid the foundation for the modern internet. Initially, its purpose was to facilitate communication and data sharing between research institutions and the military.

- Encryption and Anonymity:

In the 1990s, the Cypherpunk movement emerged, advocating for strong encryption and privacy on the internet. Pioneers such as David Chaum, Phil Zimmermann, and Tim May promoted the idea of anonymous online communication and developed encryption tools like Pretty Good Privacy (PGP).

- The Onion Routing Concept:

The concept of onion routing, which forms the basis of the Tor network, was developed by the United States Naval Research Laboratory (NRL) in the mid-1990s. Onion routing enables the anonymization of internet traffic by encrypting it and routing it through multiple layers of nodes, making it difficult to trace the origin and destination.

- The Tor Project:

The Tor Project, initially developed by Roger Dingledine, Nick Mathewson, and Paul Syverson, emerged in the early 2000s as an implementation of onion routing. It aimed to provide online privacy and circumvent censorship. The Tor network became synonymous with the dark web due to its association with hidden services and anonymous browsing.

- Silk Road and the Darknet Markets:

In 2011, the Silk Road, an online marketplace for illicit goods, gained notoriety. Operated by Ross Ulbricht (known as "Dread Pirate Roberts"), it utilized Tor and Bitcoin for anonymous transactions. Silk Road's prominence highlighted the potential of the dark web for illicit activities and attracted considerable media attention.

- Evolution and Expansion:

Over time, the dark web has continued to evolve and expand with the emergence of alternative darknet networks like I2P and Freenet. These networks offered their own variations of anonymity and services, further diversifying the dark web landscape.

It is important to recognize that while the technologies and developments mentioned above laid the groundwork for the dark web, its evolution and growth are the result of contributions from various individuals, communities, and technological advancements. The dark web's origins reflect the complex interplay between privacy concerns, technological innovation, and the darker side of human activities online.

Debunking misconceptions: Separating fact from fiction

Fact and fiction often intertwine when it comes to discussions about the dark web. It is crucial to separate the reality from the myths and misconceptions that surround this hidden part of the internet. Let's explore some key points to distinguish fact from fiction:

- Fact: Anonymity and Privacy

The dark web does offer a certain level of anonymity and privacy due to the use of encryption and anonymizing technologies like Tor. It can provide a refuge for individuals seeking privacy or those living under oppressive regimes.

- Fiction: The Entire Dark Web is Illegal

While there are illegal activities taking place on the dark web, not everything on it is inherently illegal. The dark web hosts a variety of websites, forums, and services, some of which are dedicated to legitimate purposes such as anonymous communication, free speech, and research.

- Fact: Illicit Marketplaces Exist

Dark web marketplaces, such as the infamous Silk Road, have facilitated the sale of illegal goods and services, including drugs, weapons, counterfeit currencies, and stolen data. These marketplaces operate using cryptocurrencies and strive to maintain anonymity.

- Fiction: All Dark Web Users are Criminals

It is incorrect to assume that everyone using the dark web is involved in illegal activities. While there are cybercriminals and malicious actors, there are also individuals who use the dark web for legitimate reasons such as research, journalism, activism, and protection of privacy.

- Fact: Risks and Dangers

Engaging with the dark web carries risks. Users may encounter scams, malware, law enforcement operations, or become victims of cybercrime. It is important to exercise caution and take necessary precautions when accessing and navigating the dark web.

- Fiction: Red Rooms and Human Experimentation

The notion of "red rooms," where people are tortured or killed in front of a live audience, is often sensationalized in popular culture. However, there is no credible evidence to suggest the existence of such events on the dark web. Similarly, claims of widespread human experimentation are unfounded.

- Fact: Law Enforcement Efforts

Law enforcement agencies around the world are actively involved in monitoring and investigating illegal activities on the dark web. Several successful operations have led to the takedown of illicit marketplaces, arrests of cybercriminals, and the seizure of illegal assets.

When discussing the dark web, it is crucial to approach the topic with an understanding that it encompasses both illegal and legitimate activities. While it can be a source of concern and pose risks, it is essential to base discussions on accurate information rather than sensationalized portrayals.

Chapter 2: The Hidden Layers: Navigating the Underbelly

Tor, I2P, and Freenet: The key players in dark web infrastructure

Tor, I2P, and Freenet are three prominent examples of overlay networks that enable anonymity and privacy on the internet, each with its own unique characteristics and purposes. Let's explore each of them:

Tor (The Onion Router)

Tor is perhaps the most well-known and widely used anonymity network. It operates by encrypting and routing internet traffic through a series of volunteer-operated relays, thereby obfuscating the origin and destination of the data. This multi-layered routing is often referred to as "onion routing."

Tor is primarily used to access the dark web, providing a means to browse websites hosted on the .onion domain. However, it also offers anonymous access to regular websites, protecting users' privacy and evading censorship.

I2P (Invisible Internet Project)

I2P is an overlay network that focuses on secure and anonymous communication. It uses a distributed network of nodes to establish encrypted tunnels for data transfer, ensuring privacy and protecting against surveillance.

Unlike Tor, I2P is primarily designed for hidden services and anonymous peer-to-peer communication. It allows users to host websites and services within the network, making them accessible only to other I2P users. This decentralized approach contributes to the network's resilience and resistance to censorship.

Freenet

Freenet is another decentralized, peer-to-peer network that emphasizes censorship resistance and preserving freedom of speech. It operates on the principle of distributed data storage, where each participating node stores encrypted fragments of content from other nodes.

Freenet's unique feature is its focus on the preservation of anonymity, even among content publishers. By utilizing data encryption and routing through multiple nodes, Freenet strives to protect both content creators and consumers from surveillance and censorship.

While Tor, I2P, and Freenet share the common goal of providing anonymity and privacy, they differ in their architectural designs and intended use cases. Tor primarily enables access to the dark web and anonymous web browsing, while I2P and Freenet emphasize secure communication and decentralized publishing of content.

It's important to note that while these networks offer a layer of anonymity, they do not guarantee complete protection from all potential threats. Users must still exercise caution, employ secure practices, and be mindful of potential risks when navigating these networks.

Accessing the Dark Web: Understanding the tools, techniques, and precautions

When accessing the dark web, it's essential to take certain precautions to protect your privacy, security, and anonymity. Here are some tools, techniques, and precautions to consider:

- Tor Browser:

The Tor Browser is a crucial tool for accessing the dark web securely. It is specifically designed to work with the Tor network and provides built-in features to enhance privacy and anonymity.

- VPN (Virtual Private Network):

Using a reputable VPN service can add an extra layer of security and anonymity by encrypting your internet connection and hiding your IP address from prying eyes. It is recommended to connect to a VPN before accessing the Tor network.

- Tails OS:

Tails (The Amnesic Incognito Live System) is a privacy-focused operating system that runs from a USB stick or DVD. It routes all internet connections through the Tor network, enhances anonymity, and leaves no digital footprint on the host computer.

- Security Software:

Maintain up-to-date antivirus and anti-malware software on your device to protect against potential threats that may be encountered on the dark web.

- Secure Messaging:

When communicating on the dark web, use encrypted messaging applications like Signal or Wickr to ensure the confidentiality of your conversations.

- Pseudonyms and Disposable Email Addresses:

Consider using pseudonyms and disposable email addresses when registering on dark web platforms to protect your identity and minimize the risk of personal information exposure.

- OpSec (Operational Security):

Practice good OpSec by being cautious about the information you share, both online and offline. Avoid using personal or identifiable details, such as your real name, address, or phone number.

- Avoid Suspicious Links and Downloads:

Be cautious of clicking on unknown links or downloading files from untrusted sources, as they may contain malware or lead to phishing attempts.

- Separate Devices:

Consider using a separate device or a dedicated virtual machine for accessing the dark web to isolate your dark web activities from your regular online presence.

- Stay Informed:

Stay updated on the latest security practices and potential threats associated with the dark web. Engage in online communities and forums where you can learn from experienced users and share knowledge.

Remember, engaging in illegal activities on the dark web is against the law, and this information is intended for educational purposes only. It is important to abide by legal and ethical guidelines while exploring the dark web or any other part of the internet.

The Marketplace of Secrets: Exploring illicit activities, black markets, and cybercrime

The dark web has gained notoriety for hosting various black markets and being a haven for cybercrime activities. While not all activities on the dark web are illicit, it does harbour a significant amount of illegal trade and cybercrime. Here are some key aspects related to dark web black markets and cybercrime:

- Illicit Trade:

Dark web black markets provide a platform for the sale of illegal goods and services. These can include drugs, counterfeit currencies, stolen credit card information, weapons, hacking tools, forged documents, and more.

The anonymity and encryption provided by the dark web make it attractive to sellers and buyers involved in illegal trade, as it becomes challenging to track their identities or transactions.

- Drug Marketplaces:

Dark web drug marketplaces are among the most prominent and well-known aspects of the illicit trade. These marketplaces operate similarly to regular e-commerce platforms, facilitating the sale and distribution of various drugs, including narcotics, prescription medications, and designer drugs.

Cryptocurrencies, primarily Bitcoin, are commonly used for anonymous transactions in these marketplaces.

- Hacking Tools and Services:

The dark web provides a marketplace for cybercriminals to sell and exchange hacking tools, exploit kits, malware, and hacking services. These tools enable cybercriminals to launch attacks, compromise systems, steal sensitive data, and exploit vulnerabilities for financial gain.

- Stolen Data and Credentials:

Dark web forums and marketplaces are often hubs for the sale of stolen data, including personal information, login credentials, credit card details, and social security numbers. This data is typically acquired through data breaches, phishing attacks, or malware infections.

- Cybercrime-as-a-Service (CaaS):

The dark web has popularized the concept of cybercrime-as-a-service, where individuals with limited technical skills can purchase hacking services or malware tools from more experienced cybercriminals. This allows aspiring criminals to carry out attacks without requiring in-depth technical knowledge.

- DDoS-for-Hire and Botnets:

Dark web forums and marketplaces also facilitate the sale and rental of distributed denial-of-service (DDoS) attacks and botnets. Cybercriminals can rent these resources to launch large-scale attacks against targeted websites or infrastructure, causing disruption or demanding ransom payments.

It is important to note that law enforcement agencies actively monitor and investigate illegal activities on the dark web. Several notable law enforcement operations have resulted in the takedown of major dark web marketplaces, arrests of cybercriminals, and the seizure of illicit assets.

Engaging in or supporting illegal activities is against the law and highly discouraged. This information is provided solely for educational purposes to enhance understanding of the dark web's complex landscape.

Chapter 3: The Shadows Within: Dark Web Content

Illegal Trade: Drugs, weapons, counterfeit goods, and human trafficking

The dark web is known for hosting illicit activities, including the sale of drugs, weapons, counterfeit goods, and facilitating human trafficking. It is important to understand the gravity of these issues and the role the dark web plays in facilitating such activities. Here are some key points regarding these dark web phenomena:

- Drug Trade:

Dark web marketplaces provide a platform for the sale and distribution of various drugs. These marketplaces operate similarly to regular e-commerce platforms, allowing sellers and buyers to connect anonymously.

A wide range of drugs, including narcotics, prescription medications, synthetic drugs, and recreational substances, are available for purchase on the dark web. Cryptocurrencies are typically used for transactions, providing a layer of anonymity.

- Weapons:

The dark web offers a marketplace for the sale of firearms, ammunition, and other weapons. Both legally restricted weapons and illegal firearms can be found on these platforms.

Vendors often exploit loopholes in regional regulations and discreet shipping methods to facilitate the delivery of weapons purchased through dark web transactions.

- Counterfeit Goods

Dark web marketplaces are notorious for the sale of counterfeit goods, including luxury items, electronics, counterfeit currencies, passports, and identification documents.

These counterfeit goods are often of lower quality and manufactured to resemble authentic products, deceiving unsuspecting buyers.

- Human Trafficking:

The dark web can serve as a platform for the facilitation of human trafficking, including the sale of exploited individuals for various purposes, such as forced labour or sexual exploitation.

Underground forums and hidden services may provide a space for traffickers to advertise and negotiate human trafficking activities, making it more challenging for law enforcement to detect and prevent such crimes.

It is essential to understand that engaging in any illegal activities, including purchasing or facilitating the sale of drugs, weapons, counterfeit goods, or participating in human trafficking, is against the law and morally reprehensible. Law enforcement agencies worldwide are actively working to combat these illicit activities on the dark web, often collaborating with international counterparts to identify and prosecute offenders.

Raising awareness, supporting initiatives that combat these crimes, and promoting a safe and ethical digital environment are crucial steps in addressing the issues associated with the dark web.

Hacking and Cyberattacks: Unleashing the power of cybercriminals

The dark web provides a platform for cybercriminals to exchange information, sell hacking tools, and plan and coordinate cyber-attacks. Here are some key points regarding hacking and cyber-attacks on the dark web:

- Hacking Tools and Services:

Dark web marketplaces offer a wide range of hacking tools, exploit kits, malware, and hacking services for sale. These tools enable individuals with limited technical expertise to launch cyber-attacks and compromise systems.

Common hacking tools available on the dark web include keyloggers, remote access Trojans (RATs), exploit frameworks, and botnets.

- DDoS Attacks:

Distributed Denial of Service (DDoS) attacks are a prevalent form of cyber-attack. The dark web provides a platform where individuals can rent or purchase DDoS-for-hire services or botnets to launch large-scale DDoS attacks against targeted websites or services.

These attacks can disrupt online services, overwhelm servers, and cause financial losses for businesses.

- Malware and Ransomware:

Dark web marketplaces serve as hubs for the distribution and sale of malware, including ransomware. Cybercriminals can acquire and deploy this malicious software to infect systems, encrypt files, and demand ransom payments for decryption.

Ransomware-as-a-Service (RaaS) models have emerged, where individuals with limited technical skills can purchase ransomware and receive support from the creators in exchange for a percentage of the ransom payments.

- Exploit Trading:

The dark web facilitates the trading of software vulnerabilities and exploits. Individuals and groups discover, develop, and sell undisclosed vulnerabilities, zero-day exploits, and exploit kits that can be used to compromise systems and networks.

These vulnerabilities and exploits may target popular software, operating systems, or even specific hardware devices.

- Information and Data Breaches

The dark web is a marketplace for the sale and exchange of stolen data obtained through data breaches. Personal information, login credentials, credit card details, and other sensitive data are often traded and used for various malicious activities, such as identity theft or financial fraud.

It's important to note that law enforcement agencies actively monitor and investigate cybercriminal activities on the dark web. Collaboration among international law enforcement agencies and cybersecurity organizations is crucial in combating these threats and prosecuting offenders.

It is crucial to follow ethical guidelines, practice good cybersecurity hygiene, and report any suspicious or illegal activities to the appropriate authorities. Engaging in or supporting hacking and cyber-attacks is illegal and highly discouraged.

Dark Web Forums and Communities: Radical ideologies, extremism, and hidden discussions

Dark web forums and communities play a significant role in shaping the culture and discussions within the hidden corners of the internet. These forums provide a platform for individuals to share information, exchange ideas, and engage in discussions on various topics. Here are some key points regarding dark web forums and communities:

- Anonymity and Privacy:

Dark web forums prioritize anonymity, allowing users to create pseudonyms and interact without revealing their true identities. This anonymity fosters an environment where individuals feel more comfortable discussing sensitive or controversial topics.

- Discussions and Information Sharing:

Dark web forums cover a wide range of topics, including technology, hacking, privacy, politics, whistleblowing, and more. These platforms facilitate discussions, knowledge sharing, and the exchange of information that might not be accessible or openly discussed in other online spaces.

- Radical Ideologies and Extremism:

Some dark web forums serve as gathering places for individuals with radical ideologies, including extremist groups and individuals. These platforms provide a space for like-minded individuals to discuss and promote their beliefs away from the scrutiny of traditional online platforms.

- Marketplace Feedback and Reviews:

Dark web marketplaces often have associated forums where buyers and sellers can leave feedback and reviews. This feedback helps build trust within the marketplace and assists users in making informed decisions regarding their purchases.

- Whistleblowing and Activism:

Dark web forums can serve as platforms for whistleblowers, activists, and journalists who seek to expose secrets or share sensitive information. These spaces offer a level of anonymity and security that can protect those who wish to disclose information while avoiding potential reprisals.

- Creepypastas and Horror Stories:

Dark web forums and communities are known for their contributions to the genre of creepypastas, which are horror stories, urban legends, or creepy tales shared online. These stories often revolve around mysterious dark web experiences, adding to the intrigue and mythology surrounding the hidden parts of the internet.

- Marketplace Vendor Communications:

Dark web marketplaces often have associated forums where buyers and vendors can communicate privately. These private communications allow buyers to ask questions, negotiate terms, and discuss transactions securely.

It is important to note that while dark web forums provide a platform for various discussions and communities, not all content and discussions within these spaces are legal or ethical. Illegal activities, harassment, hate speech, and discussions promoting harm should be condemned and reported to the appropriate authorities.

It is crucial to approach the dark web and its forums with caution, adhering to legal and ethical guidelines, and respecting the privacy and rights of others.

Chapter 4: Anonymity vs. Accountability: The Dark Web's Tug of War

Cryptocurrency: The lifeblood of the Dark Web economy

Cryptocurrency plays a significant role in facilitating transactions on the dark web. The pseudonymous and decentralized nature of cryptocurrencies makes them a preferred choice for transactions involving illicit goods and services. Here are some key points regarding the use of cryptocurrencies on the dark web:

- Bitcoin Dominance:

Bitcoin has traditionally been the most widely accepted and commonly used cryptocurrency on the dark web. Its popularity can be attributed to its established infrastructure, wide adoption, and relatively high level of acceptance among dark web marketplaces and vendors.

- Anonymity and Pseudonymity:

Cryptocurrencies provide a certain level of anonymity and pseudonymity on the dark web. While transactions are recorded on the blockchain, participants can use pseudonymous wallet addresses and take additional steps to enhance privacy, such as coin mixing services (also known as tumblers) that obscure transaction trails.

- Monero and Privacy Coins:

Monero and other privacy-focused cryptocurrencies have gained popularity on the dark web due to their enhanced privacy features. These coins utilize technologies such as ring

33

signatures, stealth addresses, and confidential transactions to provide greater anonymity and obfuscate transaction details.

- Escrow Services:

Dark web marketplaces often employ escrow services to facilitate secure transactions. Cryptocurrencies are used to fund the escrow, ensuring that funds are held until the buyer confirms the receipt and satisfaction of the purchased goods or services. This provides a level of trust and protection for both buyers and sellers.

- Volatility and Conversion:

Cryptocurrencies, including Bitcoin, can be subject to significant price volatility. Dark web marketplaces may factor in this volatility when pricing goods or services or may offer conversion services to stabilize the value of transactions during the purchasing process.

- Law Enforcement Concerns

Cryptocurrencies present challenges for law enforcement agencies when investigating and tracing illicit activities on the dark web. While blockchain analysis techniques can be used to identify patterns and track transactions, the anonymity and complexity of cryptocurrencies can make it difficult to attribute transactions to specific individuals.

It is important to note that cryptocurrencies have many legitimate uses and are widely adopted for legal and everyday transactions. However, their association with the dark web and illicit activities should not overshadow their broader applications and the positive aspects of blockchain technology.

Engaging in illegal activities, including using cryptocurrencies for illegal purposes, is against the law. It is important to adhere to legal and ethical guidelines and use cryptocurrencies responsibly.

Law Enforcement and Dark Web Investigations: Challenges and successes

Law enforcement agencies around the world recognize the significance of the dark web in facilitating illegal activities, and they have made efforts to investigate and combat criminal operations on these platforms. Here are some key points regarding law enforcement and dark web investigations:

- Collaboration and International Cooperation:

Dark web investigations often require collaboration among law enforcement agencies at local, national, and international levels. Sharing information, intelligence, and expertise is crucial in combating transnational cybercrime and illicit activities.

- Infiltration and Undercover Operations

Law enforcement agencies may employ undercover officers or agents who pose as buyers or sellers on dark web marketplaces to gather evidence and gain insights into criminal networks. These operations can help identify and apprehend individuals involved in illegal activities.

- Blockchain Analysis:

Blockchain analysis techniques are employed by law enforcement agencies to track and trace cryptocurrency transactions on the dark web. While the anonymity of cryptocurrencies can pose challenges, patterns and connections within the blockchain can be analysed to identify addresses, transactions, and potentially link them to individuals.

- Dark Web Intelligence Gathering:

Law enforcement agencies actively monitor dark web forums, marketplaces, and communities to gather intelligence on emerging threats, criminal activities, and potential targets. This intelligence can aid in proactive investigations and identifying individuals engaged in illegal activities.

- Seizures and Takedowns:

Law enforcement agencies have conducted numerous operations to seize and take down dark web marketplaces, disrupting illicit activities and arresting individuals involved in cybercrime and illegal trade. These operations involve coordination between various agencies, including cybercrime units, special task forces, and international partners.

- Training and Expertise:

Law enforcement agencies invest in specialized training and develop expertise in dark web investigations. This includes understanding the technical aspects of the dark web, encryption technologies, cryptocurrency analysis, and the methodologies used by cybercriminals.

- Legal Challenges and Jurisdiction

Dark web investigations often face legal challenges due to jurisdictional complexities, varying laws, and the global nature of cybercrime. Law enforcement agencies must navigate legal frameworks, obtain necessary warrants, and work within the boundaries of international cooperation agreements.

It is important to note that while law enforcement agencies strive to combat illegal activities on the dark web, the anonymous nature of these platforms presents ongoing challenges. It requires continuous adaptation and collaboration to stay ahead of cybercriminals and effectively address the complexities associated with dark web investigations.

Reporting any suspicious or illegal activities observed on the dark web to the appropriate law enforcement agencies is crucial in assisting their efforts to maintain a safer digital environment.

Privacy Concerns: Balancing individual liberties and security in the digital age

Privacy concerns on the dark web are complex and multifaceted. While the dark web can provide a certain level of anonymity and privacy, it is important to understand the risks and limitations involved. Here are some key points regarding privacy concerns on the dark web:

- User Anonymity:

The dark web employs technologies like Tor, I2P, and Freenet to help users maintain anonymity by concealing their IP addresses and physical locations. This can be beneficial for individuals seeking privacy, such as whistleblowers, activists, or those living under oppressive regimes.

- Pseudonymity:

Dark web users often adopt pseudonyms or aliases, which provide a layer of anonymity when engaging in discussions, transactions, or other activities. Pseudonyms can help protect the identity of users and prevent their real-world personas from being linked to their online actions.

- Encryption and Security:

The dark web relies on encryption techniques to secure communication and data transmission. This encryption helps protect sensitive information from being intercepted or accessed by unauthorized parties.

- Dark Web Marketplaces

Dark web marketplaces often employ features such as escrow services, where funds are held in a secure manner until both parties are satisfied with the transaction. This helps protect the financial privacy of buyers and sellers.

- Trust and Reputation:

Dark web marketplaces and forums often have reputation systems in place, allowing users to rate and provide feedback on sellers or buyers. This helps build trust and allows participants to make informed decisions based on the reputation of other users.

- OpSec and Personal Security:

Users must practice good operational security (OpSec) when accessing the dark web. This includes taking precautions to protect personal information, avoiding sharing identifying details, and using secure technologies to minimize the risk of data breaches or exposure.

However, it is crucial to recognize the limitations and risks associated with privacy on the dark web:

- User Behaviour:

Users' actions and mistakes, such as revealing personal information or engaging in illegal activities, can compromise their privacy and anonymity.

- Law Enforcement and Surveillance:

While the dark web can provide a degree of privacy, it does not guarantee protection from law enforcement agencies.

Authorities can employ various techniques, such as blockchain analysis and network monitoring, to identify and track individuals involved in illegal activities on the dark web.

- Malware and Scams:

Dark web platforms can harbour malicious actors, including scammers and vendors selling malware-infected products. Engaging with such entities can compromise privacy and security.

- Exit Nodes and Potential Vulnerabilities:

The exit nodes in the Tor network, where data exits the anonymizing network, can potentially be compromised, leading to the exposure of user data. It is important to be cautious when accessing non-HTTPS websites or sharing sensitive information on the dark web.

Privacy on the dark web should not be taken for granted, and users should understand the risks involved. It is important to exercise caution, stay informed about emerging threats, and adopt secure practices to protect privacy and security while navigating the dark web.

Chapter 5: The Psychosphere: Dark Web Culture

Creepypastas and Horror Stories: Tales from the darkest corners of the internet

Dark web creepypastas and horror stories have gained popularity as a subgenre of internet-based horror tales. Creepypastas are fictional stories, often presented as firsthand accounts or urban legends, that are shared and spread across the internet, including the dark web. Here are some key points regarding dark web creepypastas and horror stories:

- Mythology and Urban Legends:

Dark web creepypastas contribute to the mythology and mystique surrounding the hidden corners of the internet. These stories often create a sense of unease and fascination with the unknown and the potentially dangerous aspects of the dark web.

- Mysterious Experiences:

Dark web creepypastas often feature narrators who claim to have had disturbing or terrifying experiences while exploring the dark web. These experiences may involve encountering sinister individuals, stumbling upon disturbing content, or witnessing illegal activities.

- Technical and Supernatural Elements:

Dark web creepypastas blend technical aspects related to the dark web, such as encryption, anonymity, and hidden services, with supernatural or paranormal elements. This combination adds to the suspense and horror within the narratives.

- Red Rooms:

Red rooms are a recurring theme in dark web horror stories. These fictional rooms are often described as live-streamed events where participants are tortured or killed in front of a voyeuristic audience. It is important to note that there is no credible evidence to suggest the existence of real red rooms on the dark web.

- Viral Contagions and Curses:

Some dark web creepypastas revolve around the idea of encountering a viral contagion or a cursed file while browsing the dark web. These stories often involve the spreading of mysterious, malevolent entities that haunt or harm those who come into contact with them.

- Psychological Horror:

Dark web creepypastas sometimes delve into psychological horror, exploring the effects of deep web exploration on the mental well-being of the characters. These stories emphasize the sense of paranoia, dread, and helplessness that can arise from venturing into the dark web's mysterious depths.

It is important to remember that dark web creepypastas and horror stories are works of fiction. They are crafted to entertain and scare readers, often blurring the line between reality and imagination. While they contribute to the dark web's mystique, it is crucial to approach them as fictional creations rather than factual accounts.

Engaging in illegal activities or attempting to replicate events described in dark web creepypastas is both illegal and highly discouraged. It is important to adhere to legal and ethical guidelines when exploring the internet, including the dark web.

Red Rooms and Snuff Films: Urban legends or horrifying realities?

Dark web red rooms and snuff films are disturbing concepts that have been sensationalized in popular culture and urban legends. However, it is important to clarify that there is no credible evidence to support the existence of real red rooms or snuff films on the dark web. Here are some key points regarding these dark web phenomena:

- Red Rooms:

Red rooms, as described in dark web lore, are supposedly live-streamed events where individuals are tortured, abused, or killed in front of an audience. These events are often portrayed as highly sadistic and voyeuristic.

Despite their notoriety in fiction and urban legends, there is no substantiated evidence to confirm the existence of real red rooms on the dark web. Claims of participating in or accessing such events are typically fabricated or exaggerated for shock value.

- Snuff Films:

Snuff films are movies or videos that purportedly depict real acts of murder, violence, or death for the purpose of sexual gratification or entertainment. These films, if they exist, would involve actual harm or murder of individuals.

Like red rooms, there is no credible evidence to support the existence of snuff films being traded or distributed on the dark web. Any claims or rumours suggesting otherwise are often baseless or urban legends.

It is important to approach these concepts with scepticism and critical thinking. While the dark web harbours illegal activities and disturbing content, it is crucial to distinguish between reality and sensationalized narratives. The dissemination of such myths and misinformation can contribute to unnecessary fear and misunderstandings about the dark web.

It is worth noting that engaging in or seeking out illegal and harmful activities, including the production or consumption of snuff films, is a criminal offense and morally reprehensible. It is important to report any credible information regarding illegal activities to law enforcement authorities rather than perpetuating unfounded rumours or urban legends.

Whistleblowers and Activism: Uncovering secrets and exposing the truth

Whistle-blowers can play a crucial role in uncovering truth and exposing wrongdoing, even on the dark web. While the dark web is often associated with illegal activities and illicit trade, it is important to recognize that it can also serve as a platform for individuals who aim to reveal important information or shed light on hidden issues. Here are some key points regarding whistle-blowers and their role on the dark web:

- Anonymity and Protection:

Whistle-blowers on the dark web may leverage the anonymity provided by technologies like Tor or I2P to protect their identities and avoid potential reprisals. Anonymity can enable individuals to share information without fear of being identified or targeted.

- Leaking Sensitive Information:

Whistle-blowers on the dark web may choose to leak sensitive information, documents, or evidence that expose illegal activities, corruption, or unethical practices. They may do so through secure communication channels or by sharing information with trusted journalists or organizations.

- Exposure of Dark Web Activities:

Whistle-blowers who have access to insider information or are involved in illicit activities on the dark web may choose to expose those activities, shining a light on the hidden corners of the internet. Their disclosures can help law enforcement agencies and other relevant organizations take action against criminals operating on the dark web.

- Journalistic Collaboration:

Whistle-blowers who want to expose dark web activities may choose to collaborate with investigative journalists or media outlets. These collaborations can help ensure that the information is vetted, analysed, and presented in a responsible and ethical manner.

- Protecting Privacy and Safety:

Whistle-blowers should take precautions to protect their privacy and personal safety. This includes using secure communication methods, seeking legal advice, and working with trusted organizations that specialize in protecting whistle-blowers' rights and safety.

- Legal and Ethical Considerations:

Whistle-blowing on the dark web, like in any context, should adhere to legal and ethical guidelines. It is important to disclose information responsibly, respecting the privacy rights of individuals who are not involved in illegal activities.

Whistle-blowers who uncover truth on the dark web can contribute to the exposure of illegal activities, corruption, and other hidden issues. Their disclosures can assist in law enforcement efforts, raise awareness, and promote accountability and transparency. Protecting and supporting whistle-blowers is crucial to ensure that they can come forward safely and make a positive impact on society.

Chapter 6: The Future of Darkness: Emerging Trends and Challenges

AI and the Dark Web: Dystopian possibilities and ethical implications

The dark web presents dystopian possibilities and raises ethical concerns due to its potential misuse and the illicit activities that take place within its hidden corners. Here are some key points regarding the dystopian possibilities and ethical implications associated with the dark web:

- Illegal Activities and Criminal Marketplace:

The dark web facilitates the trade of illegal goods and services, including drugs, weapons, stolen data, and counterfeit goods. This thriving criminal marketplace perpetuates illicit activities and can have detrimental societal effects.

- Encrypted Communication for Criminals:

The dark web provides a platform for criminals to communicate anonymously and securely, making it more difficult for law enforcement to detect and investigate criminal activities. This can hinder the efforts to maintain law and order, protect public safety, and ensure justice.

- Cybercrime and Hacking:

The dark web serves as a hub for cybercriminals, offering tools, services, and resources for hacking, malware distribution, and cyber-attacks. This can result in financial losses, privacy breaches, and disruptions to critical infrastructure, impacting individuals, businesses, and governments.

- Exploitation and Trafficking:

The dark web can be utilized for human trafficking, including the sale and exploitation of individuals for forced labour or sexual exploitation. This poses significant ethical concerns, as it perpetuates the suffering and exploitation of vulnerable individuals.

- Privacy vs. Security Balance:

The dark web raises the ethical dilemma of balancing privacy and security. While privacy is a fundamental right, the anonymity and encryption provided by the dark web can also enable criminal activities and hinder law enforcement efforts. Striking the right balance between privacy and security becomes a challenge in addressing the ethical implications of the dark web.

- Dissemination of Harmful Content:

The dark web hosts disturbing and illegal content, including child pornography, extremist materials, and graphic violence. The dissemination of such content poses ethical concerns regarding the potential harm inflicted upon individuals, the perpetuation of exploitation, and the negative impact on society.

- Access to Information and Freedom of Speech:

While the dark web is often associated with illegal activities, it also provides a platform for individuals in oppressive regimes to access information, express dissenting opinions, and protect freedom of speech. This raises ethical considerations regarding the balance between the potential positive impact of the dark web and its potential for misuse.

It is crucial to address the dystopian possibilities and ethical implications of the dark web by promoting legal and ethical practices, supporting law enforcement efforts, raising awareness, and encouraging responsible use of technology. Collaborative efforts from governments, technology companies, and civil society can help mitigate the negative aspects associated with the dark web while preserving the benefits it may offer in terms of privacy, freedom of speech, and access to information.

Decentralization: Blockchain and the potential impact on the Dark Web

Blockchain technology has the potential to impact the dark web in various ways, both positive and negative. Here are some key points regarding the potential impact of blockchain on the dark web:

- Anonymity and Privacy:

Blockchain technology, when utilized properly, can enhance privacy and anonymity on the dark web. Privacy-focused cryptocurrencies like Monero or privacy features of other blockchain platforms can offer stronger protection against transaction tracing and surveillance.

- Enhanced Security:

The decentralized and immutable nature of blockchain can provide enhanced security for certain aspects of the dark web. For example, blockchain-based escrow systems can facilitate secure transactions and minimize the risk of fraud or disputes.

- Transparency and Auditability:

Blockchain's transparency and public ledger can potentially improve trust and accountability on the dark web. By recording transactions on the blockchain, it becomes more difficult for vendors or marketplaces to engage in fraudulent activities without leaving a trace.

- Challenges for Law Enforcement:

The pseudonymous and decentralized nature of blockchain transactions can pose challenges for law enforcement agencies investigating illegal activities on the dark web. The immutability and difficulty of identifying individuals behind blockchain transactions can make it harder to trace and attribute criminal actions.

- Smart Contracts and Decentralized Applications:

Blockchain enables the development of smart contracts and decentralized applications (DApps). These decentralized platforms can potentially provide alternative mechanisms for dark web interactions, such as decentralized marketplaces or communication channels.

- Cryptocurrency Regulation:

The rise of blockchain and cryptocurrencies has led to increased regulatory scrutiny. Regulatory efforts to monitor and regulate cryptocurrency exchanges and transactions may impact the use of cryptocurrencies on the dark web, potentially making it more challenging to conduct illicit activities.

- Blockchain Analysis:

While blockchain transactions provide a level of privacy, advancements in blockchain analysis techniques may aid law enforcement in analysing transaction patterns and identifying suspicious activities on the dark web. These analysis methods can potentially enhance the investigative capabilities of authorities.

It is important to note that the impact of blockchain on the dark web is complex and evolving. Both positive and negative implications exist, and the technology itself is neutral. The extent to which blockchain affects the dark web depends on the adoption, implementation, and countermeasures developed by various stakeholders, including law enforcement agencies, technology developers, and regulatory bodies.

Countering the Shadows: Innovations in cybersecurity and proactive measures

Innovations in cybersecurity and proactive measures are crucial for addressing the challenges posed by the dark web. Here are some key innovations and proactive measures that can enhance cybersecurity and mitigate risks on the dark web:

- Advanced Threat Intelligence:

The continuous monitoring of dark web activities, coupled with advanced threat intelligence techniques, can provide valuable insights into emerging threats, evolving cybercriminal tactics, and vulnerabilities. This information can help organizations and law enforcement agencies stay ahead of potential attacks.

- Machine Learning and AI:

Machine learning and artificial intelligence technologies can be utilized to analyse vast amounts of data and detect patterns indicative of malicious activities on the dark web. These technologies can help in the early identification of potential threats and enhance proactive measures.

- Blockchain-Based Security Solutions:

Blockchain technology can be leveraged to enhance security on the dark web. Immutable and transparent ledgers can be utilized for identity verification, secure messaging, and secure transactions, providing enhanced trust and privacy.

- Dark Web Monitoring:

Proactive monitoring of the dark web can help identify potential threats, leaked data, compromised credentials, or discussions related to cyber-attacks. Organizations can utilize specialized tools and services to monitor the dark web for any indications of potential breaches or threats targeting their systems.

- Collaboration and Information Sharing:

Collaboration between organizations, cybersecurity researchers, and law enforcement agencies is crucial for combating cybercrime on the dark web. Sharing threat intelligence, indicators of compromise, and best practices helps in strengthening collective defences and facilitates a faster response to emerging threats.

- User Awareness and Education:

Educating users about the risks and implications of the dark web is essential. Raising awareness about potential threats, safe browsing practices, and recognizing social engineering techniques can help individuals avoid falling victim to scams, phishing attempts, or malware infections associated with the dark web.

- Responsible Vulnerability Disclosure:

Encouraging responsible vulnerability disclosure helps ensure that security flaws identified on the dark web or related platforms are reported to the appropriate entities. This allows for timely remediation, reducing the potential for exploitation by cybercriminals.

- Proactive Law Enforcement Operations:

Law enforcement agencies engaging in proactive operations to infiltrate criminal networks, gather intelligence, and take down illicit marketplaces or forums on the dark web are crucial in disrupting cybercriminal activities and promoting a safer online environment.

These innovations and proactive measures are essential for strengthening cybersecurity and combating the risks posed by the dark web. By adopting a proactive approach and leveraging technological advancements, it is possible to mitigate threats, protect sensitive information, and enhance overall security.

Chapter 7: Ethics, Morality, and the Dark Web

The debate on freedom of expression versus harm: Analysing the ethical dilemmas

The presence of freedom of expression and the potential for harm on the dark web present complex and challenging ethical considerations. Here are some key points regarding freedom of expression and harm on the dark web:

- Freedom of Expression:

The dark web, like the broader internet, can provide a platform for individuals to exercise their freedom of expression, especially in regions where freedom of speech is restricted. It can allow people to express dissenting opinions, share information, or engage in discussions without fear of censorship or reprisals.

- Protection of Vulnerable Individuals:

While freedom of expression is an important value, it is essential to balance it with the protection of vulnerable individuals. The dark web can host harmful and illegal content, including child pornography, extremist materials, or guides promoting violence. These activities pose significant harm and ethical concerns that outweigh the value of unrestricted expression.

- Illegal Activities and Harmful Content:

The dark web is known for hosting illegal activities, including drug trade, human trafficking, and cybercrime. These activities cause real-world harm and negatively impact individuals and society. The potential harm inflicted through such activities should be considered when evaluating the balance between freedom of expression and the need to prevent harm.

- Ethical Responsibility:

Individuals accessing or participating in the dark web have an ethical responsibility to ensure they do not contribute to or enable harmful activities. Engaging in illegal activities, disseminating harmful content, or supporting criminal enterprises on the dark web is unethical and can have serious consequences.

- Legal and Regulatory Considerations:

Different countries have varying laws and regulations regarding freedom of expression and online content. Activities that are legal in one jurisdiction may be illegal in another. It is important to respect and abide by the legal frameworks governing online behaviour and content, regardless of the dark web or clearnet.

- Technology and Design Choices:

The design and architecture of the dark web platforms can influence the balance between freedom of expression and harm. Developers have a responsibility to consider the potential consequences of their technology choices and implement safeguards to prevent or limit harmful activities on their platforms.

- Law Enforcement and Safety:

Law enforcement agencies play a crucial role in monitoring and investigating illegal activities on the dark web. Their efforts aim to protect individuals and society from harm. Collaboration between law enforcement agencies and technology companies is vital in addressing the challenges associated with the dark web.

It is important to strike a balance between the promotion of freedom of expression and the prevention of harm. Society must continuously evaluate and adapt legal, ethical, and technological measures to mitigate risks and ensure a safe and responsible online environment.

Dark Web vigilantism: Heroes or vigilantes?

Dark web vigilantism refers to individuals or groups taking the law into their own hands and engaging in acts of perceived justice or retribution on the dark web. Here are some key points regarding dark web vigilantism:

- Unregulated Justice:

Dark web vigilantism bypasses legal systems and due process, with individuals or groups assuming the roles of judge, jury, and sometimes even executioner. They seek to enforce their own version of justice outside of established legal frameworks.

- Personal Beliefs and Motivations:

Dark web vigilantism is often driven by personal beliefs, moral convictions, or a desire for revenge. These individuals or groups feel compelled to take action against those they perceive as wrongdoers or offenders.

- Lack of Oversight and Accountability:

Dark web vigilantism lacks oversight and accountability mechanisms. Actions taken by vigilantes may lead to unintended consequences, including harm to innocent individuals, privacy breaches, or the escalation of violence.

- Ethical and Legal Concerns:

Dark web vigilantism raises ethical concerns as it can result in a violation of individuals' rights, privacy, and due process. It can also perpetuate a cycle of violence and revenge rather than seeking long-term solutions through the legal system.

- Potential for Abuse and Injustice:

Dark web vigilantism is susceptible to abuse, manipulation, and the potential for misguided actions. False accusations or mistaken identities can lead to innocent individuals being targeted and harmed, exacerbating the risks associated with vigilante justice.

- Challenges for Law Enforcement

Dark web vigilantism poses challenges for law enforcement agencies. Identifying and prosecuting vigilantes can be difficult due to the anonymity and encryption provided by the dark web, potentially hindering efforts to maintain law and order.

- Legal and Ethical Alternatives:

While there may be frustrations with perceived gaps in the legal system, it is important to address concerns through legal and ethical means. Encouraging responsible reporting, supporting law enforcement efforts, and advocating for reforms within the legal system are more appropriate avenues for seeking justice.

It is important to recognize that dark web vigilantism is not a justifiable or sustainable approach to addressing societal issues. The rule of law, due process, and an equitable legal system are essential for upholding justice and protecting individual rights. Collaborative efforts between individuals, communities, and law enforcement are necessary to address grievances within the boundaries of the legal system.

Societal implications: How the Dark Web shapes our offline world

The dark web can have an impact on the offline world in various ways, influencing both individuals and society as a whole. Here are some key points regarding how the dark web can shape the offline world:

- Illicit Trade and Criminal Activities:

The dark web facilitates illegal trade, including the sale of drugs, weapons, stolen data, and counterfeit goods. This underground economy can have real-world consequences, contributing to drug addiction, violence, financial fraud, and the spread of illicit goods in society.

- Cybersecurity Threats:

The dark web serves as a platform for cybercriminals to exchange information, sell hacking tools, and coordinate cyber-attacks. These activities pose significant cybersecurity threats to individuals, businesses, and even critical infrastructure, potentially causing financial losses, data breaches, and disruptions in the offline world.

- Radicalization and Extremism:

The dark web can play a role in the radicalization process by providing an environment for extremist ideologies to flourish. Online communities on the dark web can amplify and spread extremist content, influencing individuals and potentially leading to offline acts of violence or terrorism.

- Privacy and Encryption Advocacy:

The dark web's emphasis on privacy and encryption has influenced conversations and debates in the offline world regarding individual privacy rights, data protection, and government surveillance. It has contributed to increased awareness and discussions surrounding online privacy and the need for secure communication channels.

- Whistleblowing and Activism:

The dark web provides a platform for whistleblowers, activists, and journalists to share sensitive information, expose secrets, and promote transparency. Their revelations on the dark web can have significant offline consequences, leading to investigations, public debates, policy changes, or legal actions.

- Law Enforcement Efforts and Legislation:

The challenges posed by the dark web have prompted law enforcement agencies to adapt their strategies and invest in cybercrime investigations. Legislation related to cybersecurity, online crime, and digital privacy has also been shaped by the impact of the dark web on the offline world.

- Inspiration for Fiction and Pop Culture:

The dark web's mysterious and illicit nature has inspired various forms of media, including books, movies, and TV shows. These portrayals shape public perceptions and generate interest in the dark web, influencing how individuals perceive and interact with it both online and offline.

It is important to recognize that the dark web is just one aspect of the broader internet landscape. While it can have significant offline consequences, it is essential to approach discussions and actions related to the dark web in a responsible and ethical manner. Collaborative efforts from governments, technology companies, and civil society are needed to address the negative impacts of the dark web and promote a safer online and offline environment.

Chapter 8: The Light Beyond: Navigating the Dark Web Safely

Digital hygiene: Protecting yourself from cyber threats

Protecting yourself from threats on the dark web requires a combination of proactive measures and cautious behaviour. Here are some key steps you can take to enhance your security and minimize risks:

- Maintain Updated Security Software

Ensure that your devices, including computers and smartphones, have up-to-date antivirus software, firewalls, and anti-malware tools. Regularly update these security solutions to protect against known threats.

- Use Secure and Private Connections:

When accessing the dark web, use a reliable virtual private network (VPN) to encrypt your internet connection and hide your IP address. This adds an extra layer of security and privacy.

- Be Cautious with Personal Information:

Avoid sharing personal information, such as your real name, address, or financial details, on the dark web or any untrusted platforms. Limit the information you provide to the absolute minimum necessary.

- Create Strong and Unique Passwords:

Use strong, complex passwords for all your online accounts, including those associated with the dark web. Avoid using the same password across multiple platforms. Consider using a password manager to securely store and generate strong passwords.

- Educate Yourself about Phishing and Social Engineering:

Be aware of phishing attempts and social engineering techniques used to trick individuals into revealing sensitive information. Exercise caution when clicking on links or downloading files from untrusted sources, as they may contain malware or lead to phishing scams.

- Practice Safe Browsing Habits:

Be cautious when navigating the dark web. Stick to reputable and verified marketplaces or forums. Avoid clicking on suspicious links, downloading files from unknown sources, or engaging in activities that may expose you to potential risks.

- Regularly Update Software and Patches:

Keep your operating system, web browsers, and other software applications updated with the latest security patches. Software updates often include bug fixes and security enhancements that protect against known vulnerabilities.

- Regularly Monitor Your Financial Accounts:

Regularly review your bank and credit card statements for any unauthorized transactions. Report any suspicious activity to your financial institution immediately.

- Stay Informed and Seek Expert Advice:

Stay updated on emerging threats and best practices for online security. Seek advice from trusted sources, such as cybersecurity experts or law enforcement agencies, to ensure you have accurate information and guidance.

- Report Illegal Activities:

If you come across illegal activities or content on the dark web, report it to the appropriate law enforcement agencies. Your cooperation can contribute to efforts in combating cybercrime and maintaining a safer online environment.

It is important to note that accessing the dark web can pose legal and ethical risks. It is strongly advised to comply with the laws of your jurisdiction and use the dark web responsibly and within legal boundaries.

Building digital resilience: Education and awareness

Education and awareness about the dark web are essential for individuals to understand its nature, risks, and potential implications. Here are some key points regarding education and awareness of the dark web:

- Understand What the Dark Web Is:

Educate yourself about the dark web, its structure, and how it differs from the surface web. Learn about the technologies used, such as Tor, I2P, or Freenet, and their implications for anonymity and privacy.

- Risks and Dangers:

Familiarize yourself with the potential risks and dangers associated with the dark web, including illegal activities, cybercrime, scams, malware, and exposure to explicit or disturbing content. Understanding these risks can help you make informed decisions and protect yourself.

- Responsible Use:

Promote responsible use of the internet, including the dark web. Emphasize the importance of adhering to legal and ethical guidelines, respecting the rights and privacy of others, and avoiding engagement in illegal activities.

- Privacy and Security Measures:

Educate individuals about privacy and security measures they can take to protect themselves online, such as using secure passwords, enabling two-factor authentication, employing VPNs, and being cautious with personal information.

- Recognizing Social Engineering Techniques:

Raise awareness about social engineering techniques used by cybercriminals to manipulate and deceive individuals. Help people recognize common tactics such as phishing, spear-phishing, and social media manipulation, which can be used to target individuals on the dark web.

- Reporting Suspicious or Illegal Activities:

Encourage individuals to report any suspicious or illegal activities they encounter on the dark web to the appropriate law enforcement agencies. Reporting can contribute to efforts in combating cybercrime and minimizing the harm caused by illicit activities.

- Digital Literacy and Critical Thinking:

Promote digital literacy skills and critical thinking to help individuals assess the credibility and reliability of information encountered on the dark web or other online platforms. This includes evaluating sources, fact-checking, and being aware of misinformation or false claims.

- Open Dialogue and Discussions:

Foster open dialogue and discussions about the dark web within communities, schools, and workplaces. Encourage people to ask questions, share concerns, and seek reliable information to foster a better understanding of the dark web and its implications.

- Collaboration with Law Enforcement and Cybersecurity Experts:

Collaborate with law enforcement agencies, cybersecurity experts, and organizations specializing in online safety and security to provide educational resources, workshops, or training programs on the risks and precautions associated with the dark web.

- Continuous Learning and Adaptation:

The landscape of the dark web is constantly evolving. Encourage individuals to stay updated on emerging threats, cybersecurity best practices, and legal frameworks to adapt their knowledge and behaviours accordingly.

By promoting education and awareness of the dark web, individuals can make informed decisions, protect themselves and their privacy, and contribute to a safer online environment.

Closing the gap: Working together to combat the dark underbelly of the internet

Combatting the dark underbelly of the internet, including the dark web, requires a multi-faceted approach involving various stakeholders. Here are some key strategies to consider:

- Strengthen Law Enforcement Efforts:

Provide adequate resources and training to law enforcement agencies to investigate and prosecute cybercrime and illegal activities on the dark web. Foster international collaboration to enhance coordination in addressing transnational cybercrime.

- Enhanced Legislation and Regulations:

Develop and enforce comprehensive laws and regulations that address cybercrime, data protection, and online privacy. This includes legislation specific to the dark web, empowering authorities to take appropriate action against illegal activities.

- Collaboration with Technology Companies:

Foster collaboration between governments, law enforcement agencies, and technology companies to develop tools and technologies that enhance security, detect illegal activities, and protect users from harm on the dark web.

- Public-Private Partnerships:

Encourage partnerships between governments, law enforcement agencies, and private sector entities to share information, intelligence, and best practices for combating cybercrime on the dark web. Collaboration can lead to more effective responses and greater impact.

- Education and Awareness:

Promote education and awareness programs targeting individuals, communities, and organizations about the risks, dangers, and ethical implications associated with the dark web. Encourage responsible use of the internet and provide guidance on how to identify and report illegal activities.

- Technological Solutions:

Invest in research and development of advanced technologies that can aid in detecting and preventing illegal activities on the dark web. This includes advancements in blockchain analysis, machine learning, and artificial intelligence for identifying and tracking criminal behaviour.

- International Cooperation:

Foster international cooperation and information sharing among governments, law enforcement agencies, and international organizations to combat cybercrime and illicit activities on the dark web. Develop frameworks for extradition and cooperation in investigating and prosecuting criminals operating across borders.

- Targeting Financial Infrastructure:

Disrupt the financial infrastructure that supports illegal activities on the dark web by targeting money laundering networks, enhancing cryptocurrency regulations, and promoting cooperation between financial institutions and law enforcement agencies.

- Ethical Hacking and Vulnerability Disclosure:

Encourage responsible ethical hacking and vulnerability disclosure practices to identify and mitigate vulnerabilities in dark web platforms. Offer protections and incentives for security researchers to report vulnerabilities rather than exploiting them.

- Public Support and Reporting

Encourage individuals to report suspicious activities, illegal content, and instances of cybercrime encountered on the dark web to the appropriate authorities. Public support and cooperation are essential in combating the dark underbelly of the internet.

It is important to note that combating the dark underbelly of the internet is a challenging and ongoing process. Continuous collaboration, adaptation to emerging threats, and a balanced approach that respects privacy rights and the rule of law are crucial to effectively address the issues associated with the dark web.

Epilogue: Illuminating the Shadows: Reflections on the Dark Web

The lasting impact of the Dark Web on society and the internet

The dark web has had a lasting impact on society and the internet, shaping various aspects of both. Here are some key points regarding the lasting impact of the dark web:

- Technology and Privacy:

The dark web has influenced the development of technologies that prioritize privacy and anonymity, such as the use of encryption, decentralized networks, and anonymous browsing tools. This has led to increased awareness and demand for privacy-focused technologies in the mainstream.

- Cybersecurity Awareness:

The existence of the dark web and its association with cybercrime has raised awareness about the importance of cybersecurity. Individuals, organizations, and governments have become more vigilant and proactive in protecting their online presence and sensitive information.

- Criminal Innovation:

The dark web has served as a breeding ground for innovation in cybercrime. Criminal actors on the dark web have been at the forefront of developing new hacking techniques, malware, and anonymity tools. Their activities have pushed law enforcement agencies and cybersecurity professionals to continually adapt and enhance their capabilities.

- Legal and Legislative Responses:

The dark web's illicit activities have prompted governments around the world to develop and enforce laws and regulations to combat cybercrime, protect privacy, and regulate cryptocurrencies. These legal responses aim to address the challenges posed by the dark web and maintain law and order in the digital realm.

- Challenges for Law Enforcement:

The dark web presents significant challenges for law enforcement agencies due to its anonymous nature and use of encryption. It has required authorities to develop new investigative techniques, forge partnerships with international counterparts, and invest in specialized training and resources to effectively combat cybercrime on the dark web.

- Evolving Criminal Landscape

The dark web has shaped the criminal landscape, enabling the growth of various illicit markets and underground economies. It has facilitated the trade of illegal goods and services, including drugs, weapons, stolen data, and counterfeit goods. The consequences of this criminal activity have had lasting societal impacts.

- Anonymity vs. Surveillance Debate:

The dark web has contributed to ongoing debates surrounding the balance between privacy and surveillance. It has sparked discussions about the role of governments, technology companies, and individuals in preserving privacy rights while preventing illicit activities and maintaining public safety.

- Media and Cultural Influence:

The dark web has captivated the popular imagination, influencing media depictions, literature, and entertainment. It has inspired stories, movies, and TV shows that explore the dark side of the internet and its potential implications for society. These cultural influences contribute to the ongoing dialogue and perceptions surrounding the dark web.

- Ethical Considerations:

The existence of the dark web raises ethical considerations regarding the boundaries of online behaviour, freedom of expression, and the responsibility of technology providers and users. It prompts discussions about the ethical implications of privacy, anonymity, and the role of individuals and society in combating illicit activities online.

The lasting impact of the dark web on society and the internet underscores the need for ongoing dialogue, collaboration, and regulation to ensure the responsible use of technology, protect privacy, and address the challenges posed by criminal activities in the digital realm.

Lessons learned and future considerations

Predicting the future of the dark web is challenging due to its ever-evolving nature and the rapid pace of technological advancements. However, several trends and possibilities may shape its future:

- Technological Advances

As technology continues to advance, the dark web may see improvements in encryption, anonymity, and decentralized networks. These advancements could make it even more challenging for law enforcement agencies to track and monitor illicit activities.

- Increased Law Enforcement Efforts:

Governments and law enforcement agencies worldwide are investing in cybercrime units and developing specialized capabilities to combat illegal activities on the dark web. This trend is likely to continue, potentially leading to more successful operations targeting dark web marketplaces and criminal networks.

- Regulation and Legislative Measures

Governments may introduce stricter regulations and legislation to tackle the dark web's illicit activities. This could involve enhanced cryptocurrency regulations, increased surveillance capabilities, and international cooperation to dismantle criminal networks operating on the dark web.

- Evolving Criminal Tactics:

Cybercriminals will continue to adapt and evolve their tactics to evade law enforcement efforts. This could involve the use of new encryption methods, decentralized marketplaces, or emerging technologies such as artificial intelligence or blockchain-based anonymity.

- Dark Web Fragmentation:

The dark web may experience fragmentation as law enforcement operations disrupt existing marketplaces and forums. This could result in a more dispersed and decentralized dark web landscape, making it harder for users to find trusted platforms and increasing the risks of scams and fraud.

- Rising Privacy Concerns:

Ongoing debates around privacy and surveillance may impact the dark web. Stricter regulations and surveillance measures may lead to a shift in user behaviour, with individuals seeking even more secure and private alternatives to protect their online activities.

- Collaboration and Innovation:

Collaboration between law enforcement agencies, cybersecurity researchers, and technology companies may drive innovation in combating dark web activities. New tools, techniques, and partnerships may emerge to tackle emerging threats and protect individuals and organizations from the risks associated with the dark web.

- Increased Public Awareness:

As the dark web continues to be a subject of media coverage and public interest, awareness and understanding about its risks and implications may grow. This could lead to more informed individuals who take proactive measures to protect themselves online and report illegal activities.

It is important to note that while efforts to combat the dark web's illicit activities will continue, it is unlikely to disappear entirely. The dark web's nature of anonymity and the demand for illicit goods and services suggest its persistence, albeit in an evolving form. Continued collaboration, technological advancements, and a comprehensive approach involving various stakeholders are crucial in shaping the future of the dark web and minimizing its negative impacts on society.

Striving for a brighter, safer digital future

Achieving a safer digital future on the dark web requires concerted efforts and collaboration among various stakeholders. Here are some key steps that can contribute to creating a safer environment:

- Enhanced Encryption and Privacy Measures

Continue developing and implementing robust encryption and privacy measures to protect user identities and communication on the dark web. Encourage the adoption of privacy-focused technologies and tools that prioritize security and anonymity.

- Responsible Technology Development:

Technology developers should prioritize security and user safety when designing platforms and tools for the dark web. Conduct regular security audits, address vulnerabilities promptly, and adhere to ethical guidelines to prevent misuse of technology.

- Improved User Education and Awareness

Educate users about the risks, potential harm, and responsible practices associated with the dark web. Promote awareness about phishing, scams, and other cyber threats. Encourage individuals to seek reliable sources of information and exercise caution while engaging with the dark web.

- Collaborative Law Enforcement Efforts

Enhance collaboration between law enforcement agencies, technology companies, and international organizations to detect and disrupt criminal activities on the dark web. Foster intelligence sharing, joint investigations, and coordinated operations to target key actors and dismantle illicit networks.

- Targeted Regulation and Legislation:

Develop targeted regulations and legislation that specifically address the challenges posed by the dark web. Strive for a balance between privacy rights, freedom of expression, and the need to prevent and prosecute illegal activities. Foster international cooperation to harmonize laws and improve cross-border enforcement.

- Ethical Hacking and Responsible Vulnerability Disclosure:

Encourage ethical hackers and cybersecurity researchers to actively identify vulnerabilities on dark web platforms and report them responsibly. Establish channels for responsible vulnerability disclosure to address security gaps and improve overall system resilience.

- Strengthen Cryptocurrency Regulations:

Develop and enforce robust regulations around cryptocurrencies to prevent their misuse for illicit activities on the dark web. Encourage transparency and accountability within the cryptocurrency ecosystem, including exchanges and transactions.

- Public-Private Partnerships

Foster partnerships between governments, private sector entities, academia, and civil society organizations to address the challenges of the dark web collectively. Encourage knowledge sharing, research collaboration, and the development of innovative solutions.

- International Cooperation:

Strengthen international cooperation and information sharing among governments and law enforcement agencies to effectively combat cybercrime on the dark web. Develop frameworks for extradition, mutual legal assistance, and coordination in investigating and prosecuting criminals operating across borders.

- Continuous Monitoring and Adaptation:

Continuously monitor the evolving landscape of the dark web, emerging technologies, and criminal tactics. Adapt strategies and responses to effectively address new threats and challenges. Foster a culture of continuous improvement and learning.

Creating a safer digital future on the dark web requires a holistic approach that combines technological advancements, law enforcement efforts, user education, and international collaboration. By working together, it is possible to mitigate risks, protect individuals and organizations, and promote responsible use of the dark web.

Milton Keynes UK
Ingram Content Group UK Ltd.
UKHW020750210823
427162UK00013B/247